CONTEMPORARY LIVING
IN THE MIDDLE EAST

الحياة المعاصرة في الشرق الأوسط

BETA-PLUS

Contents

5	Foreword	
6-21	Giacuzzo Design Studio	MV64 Home
22-41	H+A	The Ritz-Carlton Villas al Wadi Desert
42-55	Neeshay Nouman (The Niche Corner)	Arabian Ranches Home in Dubai
56-69	Tristan Du Plessis	Sān Beach Dubai
70-81	Amphora	The New Amphora Headquarters in Dubai
82-95	HI Projects Design Studio	Rixos Hotel Residence Apartment
96-109	Abboud Malak	One Palm Residence 1403
110-123	archiSENSE	House ar - Details Within Walls
124-139	VSHD Design	The Pool House
140-153	XO Atelier - Augustine Wong	A Minimalist Sanctuary in Dubai
154-161	NAQSH Architecture	Break Al Qana
162-175	Hana Hakim	Casa Amal, Dubai
176-191	Kengo Kuma	St Regis Red Sea Resort, Saudi Arabia
192-205	Custom No.9	Casa Maya
206-221	Etereo	Burj Khalifa Rubino Penthouse
222-247	MMA Projects	Villa ABK
248-253	A Tribute to the Best Architecture & Interior Photographers in the Middle East	
255	Acknowledgments	

Miriam Llano. Portrait by Oscar Munart

Foreword

In a region where history intertwines with modernity, "**Contemporary Living in the Middle East**" presents a stunning collection of visionary works by seventeen renowned architects and designers.

This book is a celebration of the transformative architecture and design projects that have redefined residential living in the Emirates and Saudi Arabia. Each project showcased within these pages exemplifies the remarkable fusion of traditional Middle Eastern aesthetics with contemporary global influences.

From the soaring skylines of Dubai to a Red Sea Resort in Saudi Arabia, the projects featured here reflect a deep respect for cultural heritage while embracing innovation and modern functionality. The architects and designers highlighted in this book have masterfully navigated the delicate balance between honoring the past and paving the way for the future. Their creations are not just structures but narratives of a region rich in history, artistry, and ingenuity.

As you journey through the pages of "**Contemporary Living in the Middle East**," you will discover homes that are sanctuaries of beauty, spaces where design meets purpose, and where global inspirations come alive. Each project stands as a testament to the vision and craftsmanship of its creator, offering a glimpse into the future of residential design in the Middle East.

This book pays tribute to the architects and designers who, with their exceptional talent and dedication, have contributed to the evolving landscape of the region. It is a homage to the timeless elegance and innovation that define contemporary living in the Middle East, celebrating the union of the region's historical richness with the boundless possibilities of modern design.

We invite you to explore these remarkable projects, to appreciate the beauty and ingenuity they represent, and to be inspired by the harmonious blend of tradition and modernity that characterizes contemporary living in the Middle East.

As the founder of Dubai-based Amphora (featured on pages 70-81 in this book), I am delighted to introduce these inspirational designers and architects.

This book also serves as an inspiration for an upcoming Amphora Series of Monographs, which will spotlight designers and architects based in the Emirates.

I hope you thoroughly enjoy the beautiful projects showcased in this book.

Miriam Llano
Amphora Founder & Managing Director

Erika Giacuzzo *Giorgia Giacuzzo*

Giacuzzo Design Studio

Giacuzzo Design Studio, founded in Italy by Architect Marco Giacuzzo has now established its first studio in the Middle East which is led by Architects & Designers Erika & Giorgia Giacuzzo.

Founded with the intent to merge the diverse experiences its founders gained from their extensive travels, the Dubai based studio sets a new benchmark for the region. A special focus is placed on bringing the renowned Italian style known for its timeless design, craftsmanship and execution.

Giacuzzo Design Studio is involved in multiple projects across the Middle East, Europe & North Africa - specializing in high end projects from Luxury Villas to Resorts.

Enhancing the natural environment with sophisticated designs that evoke a sense of tranquility while using raw materials and layers of texture to bring unique projects to life.

Erika Giacuzzo graduated in Architecture from IUAV University of Venice and subsequently attended Master 2 at the Mendrisio Academy of Architecture in Switzerland, founded by Architect Mario Botta. This allowed her to work closely with renowned figures in architecture and design such as Antonio Citterio and Aurelio Galfetti. After gaining professional experience in Lugano, Erika expanded her expertise in Beijing, Shanghai, and Hong Kong, developing a metropolitan and refined style where materiality and simplicity contribute to timeless design.

Graduated in Architecture from IUAV University of Venice, Giorgia Giacuzzo furthered her education with a Master 2 at the University of Oulu in Finland. There, she developed a passion for Nordic design and a meticulous attention to detail. This experience expanded her expertise in furniture design and furniture components. Giorgia later moved to Sydney, where she worked at prominent architectural and interior design studios developing an extensive knowledge on construction and site detailing.

www.giacuzzodesignstudio.com

MV64 Home

Presenting VILLA MV64, a timeless interior design creation by Giacuzzo Design Studio.

Established by the Italian duo Erika and Giorgia Giacuzzo, this residence embodies a refined design philosophy. Seamlessly blending soft yet defined architectural lines, the tranquil interiors evoke a sense of peace and retreat.

Drawing inspiration from nature, the interiors are crafted with natural materials and textures which echos a serene ambiance of sandy beaches and calm waters.

The gentle curves of the staircase enhance the feeling of openness while the elegant materials reflect and absorb light in a manner reminiscent of its outdoor environment - balancing monolithic design with a light composition. Unfilled Italian travertine shapes the flooring and runs through the custom joinery. Plaster textured walls surround the space creating a plethora of shadows while timber beams define the ceiling producing a delicate yet refined atmosphere.

Everything plays a role from the integrated architectural lighting to the cladded walls and timber joinery. A relaxing feeling is generated by leveraging the different neutral tones flowing through out the rooms.

VILLA MV64 offers a haven where everyday living is infused with the calm and relaxation of a coastal retreat - providing a sanctuary from the demands of modern life.

Photography: Oculis Project

David Lessard
Design Director H+A

Portrait by Anna Maria Nielsen

Stas Louca
Managing Director H+A

H+A

H+A is a Dubai-based architecture and interior design studio led by Partners Stas Louca and David Lessard specializing in healthcare, hospitality, and wellness projects.

Their design methodology is research-based, exploring all opportunities to ensure their projects are responsive, relevant, and meaningful – satisfying the client's brief while enhancing the places and communities they occupy.

They take a human-centric approach with empathy towards their clients and end users, promoting wellness and sustainability in all aspects of their project designs.

H+A strive to understand what a project 'should be' with sensitivity towards context, environment, and culture. Drawing inspiration from the local vernacular, they interpret regional forms and materials to deliver projects that are modern, timeless, and 'of the place.'

https://h-a.global

The Ritz-Carlton Villas al Wadi Desert

The Ritz Carlton al Wadi Desert (Ras Al Khaimah, United Arab Emirates) is one of the UAE's most iconic resorts - situated on a desert nature reserve - an idyllic setting of undulating sand dunes and abundant wildlife.

The extension proposed by H+A consists of 8 two-bedroom villas, generously spaced and remotely located for a sense of exclusivity.

The new villas seek to retain the essences of the existing resort, while leveraging the unique desert nature and rich cultural heritage of Ras Al Khaimah to create a new unique product that compliments the current offering.

Privacy and luxury are key drivers in creating a memorable atmosphere for guests who seek to set themselves apart - with framed vistas and enhanced amenities above and beyond the comparative set in the region.

The material composition of the project will draw parallels to the surrounding context while introducing a new material dialogue of clean lines and bold forms that blur the intersection between desert and built form.

Photography: Oculis Project

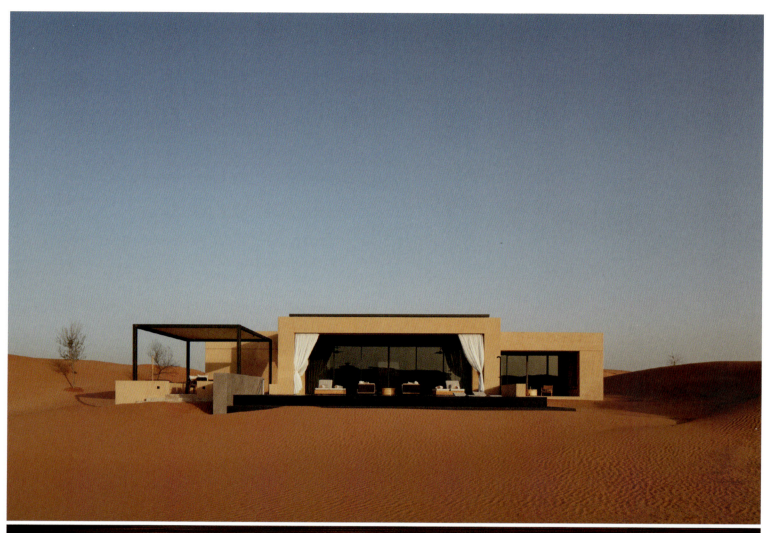

Neeshay Nouman (The Niche Corner)

Neeshay Nouman was immersed in the world of Corporate Communications until she decided to change her career path to pursue her true passion: home interiors.

Neeshay's interest in interior design was spurred by the realization that a minimalist home setting need not be boring, bland, and plain. "Quiet luxury" became her philosophy for creating beautiful spaces.

During the Covid-19 lockdowns, the time she spent at home got her thinking, and she decided to pursue interior design full-time, going at it full throttle.

Since launching "The Niche Corner," the now Abu Dhabi-based interior designer, who moved from Sydney, has worked on numerous local and overseas projects, from Dubai to Geneva.

www.thenichecorner.com

Arabian Ranches Home in Dubai

Dubai's prestigious Arabian Ranches neighborhood recently welcomed a stunning new addition: a minimalist villa for a young couple that exudes serenity and peace.

Neeshay Nouman of The Niche Corner showcased her skills in designing this 3,500 square foot home. She reimagined the house's layout, implementing a thorough renovation.

The living and dining spaces were extended, and the kitchen was redesigned for open-plan movement. The powder bathroom was renovated, and one large bathroom was converted into two smaller ones, creating ensuites for two guest bedrooms. The primary ensuite was replanned, with new flooring and lighting installed throughout the home.

The landscaping and hardscaping were transformed, featuring a 70-year-old olive tree shipped from Spain to the UAE, overlooking the living room from outside.

The current residents believe in the saying 'happiness is in the little things,' and Nouman aimed to convey this feeling throughout the interior. She chose light, airy spaces with room for fine details. The predominantly white look contrasts beautifully with the kitchen made of pure walnut wood and copper accents. In the sitting area, she selected a large white armchair with a downy look that invites you to settle down. The black-framed windows provide the right perspective, offering just enough separation from the outside world. The carefully selected furniture flows seamlessly throughout the home.

Nouman drew her inspiration from European references, where timelessness is central. Neeshay and her team kept the palette extremely minimal, wanting to incorporate many touches of wood into the concept. This was to bring warmth and integrate the surrounding nature into the interior.

Neeshay has succeeded in creating a serene interior that perfectly reflects the energy of the young habitants.

Photography: Natelee Cocks

Tristan Du Plessis

Tristan Du Plessis is an internationally acclaimed interior architect based in Cape Town, South Africa, with offices in both Dubai and London.

Founded in 2015, his boutique design studio specializes in high-end hospitality and luxury residential projects worldwide.

Tristan Du Plessis, a renowned young designer with 10 years of experience in the hospitality design industry, has completed a portfolio of projects that includes some of the most talked-about hospitality destinations globally.

www.tristanduplessis.com

Sān Beach Dubai

SĀN Beach draws inspiration from the deep-rooted wisdom of the San people, honoring elemental rhythms and the connection between self and others. The San believed in an invisible energy, accessed through ritual, which held vibrational potency or magic power. This energy was alive, used for healing both illnesses and societal divisions, always serving as a force for good. At SĀN Beach, they aim to co-create a similar energy - one that is well-intentioned, tender, and vibrant. Through art, nourishment, music, and connection, these rituals create a resonance that lingers beyond the moment.

South African designer Tristan Du Plessis and his eponymous studio are behind the design personality of the beach club.

The restaurant is an open-plan space with a large open kitchen, utilizing art and sculpture throughout to convey the SĀN story. The design emphasizes African luxury, which Du Plessis describes as a luxurious feel created with raw and primal materials and textures. Their favorite design element is the interior's form; using curves, arches, and soft edges, the space appears as if it were molded by hand from ancient clay, offering a poetic softness and feminine feel.

The art that permeates the space is another highlight. All pieces are made in Africa, including beach sculptures by artist Jake Singer, ceramic outdoor tables handmade in Cape Town, lamps by Jan Ernst, sculptural pots by Jade Paton, and an enigmatic sculptural bench by David Krynauw. The outdoor pools, set against the sand, serve as features in themselves, offering visual refreshment.

www.sanbeachdubai.com

Photography: Natelee Cocks

Miriam Llano and her husband, Portuguese designer Frederico Cruz

Amphora

Founded in 2023 by Spanish entrepreneur and brand strategist Miriam Llano, Amphora is a Dubai-based marketing consultancy specializing in the design and architecture industry. Amphora's strength lies in its core team of seasoned professionals with expertise in PR, events, industry collaborations, and digital marketing for leading global design brands.

Amphora was created with the ultimate goal of fostering collaborations and building cross-industry networks. Its rapidly growing portfolio includes distinguished international design brands as well as renowned interior design and architecture firms. Amphora's mission is to facilitate winning alliances and harness the power of partnerships.

The name "Amphora" reflects their constant pursuit of meaning and truth. It pays homage to one of the earliest marketing innovations in history - the amphora, a uniquely shaped vase that revolutionized consumer packaging in the ancient Mediterranean by enabling efficient transportation and easy identification of precious liquids.

Miriam Llano explains, «Amphora's team is not a result of chance but of careful selection. Each member possesses a blend of design and marketing expertise. Picture a group of high-profile marketing experts with international backgrounds and local experience who breathe, live, and sleep design and architecture. It's not easy to assemble such a team, but that's what it takes to achieve what we do.»

www.beamphora.com

The New Amphora Headquarters in Dubai

In 2024, Amphora opened its new office in the Kia Flagship Building on Sheikh Zayed Road, Dubai.

Conceived to feel like home, the space is the vision of Amphora's founder, Miriam Llano, brought to life by her partner, Portuguese designer Frederico Cruz.

Cruz is an interior designer from Portugal with a Master's degree from ELISAVA, Barcelona. With over 12 years of experience in hospitality and residential design, serving in senior positions at firms like GAJ, Wilson Associates, and Ellington Properties, he is currently the Design and Architecture Director at Kerzner International.

Drawing from his diverse cultural experience coupled with an eye for cutting-edge design, he is known for delivering iconic and uniquely devised projects both regionally and internationally. Frederico's technical acumen, resulting from working in a range of sectors from residential to construction, combined with his passion for travel, has served him well in handling the sheer variety and scale of designs. Inspired by his many journeys around the world, he exceeds expectations by bringing a personal touch of authenticity and memorability to every project.

Avoiding a typical corporate setup, Amphora's new office was designed as a "luxury residence in 80 sq. m," intended to foster collaboration, inspiration, and creativity with its open plan, glass partitions, and warm, earthy tones.

Founded in 2023, Amphora has quickly established itself in the MENA region's design and architecture industry. Initially operating from a shared workspace in Dubai Design District (d3), the company's rapid growth necessitated a move to a larger, more personalized space.

"Both personally and professionally, I felt my team deserved a beautiful and inspiring space. It was equally important to have an office that reflects the high caliber of our work and the clients we represent," says Llano. "As a consultancy that lives and breathes design, our space needed to be a testament to that."

Llano enlisted the expertise of her partner, Frederico Cruz, to bring her vision to life. "Miriam wanted the team to feel like they were coming home. The space also needed to be dynamic and flexible to accommodate Amphora's daily activities," Cruz explains.

The interior design reflects Miriam's personal style of timeless elegance. It's an intimate, calm, and neutral space that immediately puts everyone at ease. Classical design elements provide a sense of familiarity, making the space relatable. There are no eccentric accents; it's simple without being minimalistic, an interplay of lines, softness, textures, and materials.

Miriam Llano and her team, who are no strangers to design, collaborated with leading industry professionals and suppliers to transform the space from shell to fit-out in a record two and a half months. Amphora's partners invested their time and energy to create bespoke furniture, contributed precious pieces from their collections, and managed the fit-out from start to finish. "The space is filled with so much goodwill that we feel the energy as soon as we open the door," confirms Llano.

The fit-out by WalkThru Contracting seamlessly integrates all design elements with impeccable attention to detail, outstanding craftsmanship, and a flawless finish. The herringbone wood flooring by Chabros, walls painted in colors from Jotun's new Canva collection, and desks and communal tables crafted from Dekton by Cosentino for a stone-inspired look all contribute to the elegant ambiance.

Blending contemporary and classic pieces, the furniture selection includes office chairs by Actiu, Hermes chairs from Brazilian design house Breton, a wooden console from Nakkash Gallery, a bespoke round table by C'est ici Design, and the meeting room table and statement lamps from Spanish brand La Nena.

Architectural lighting from Soma Studio, Vibia's creative and sleek lighting fixtures, and sound by Hidden all come together to create the perfect ambiance.

Photography: Natelee Cocks

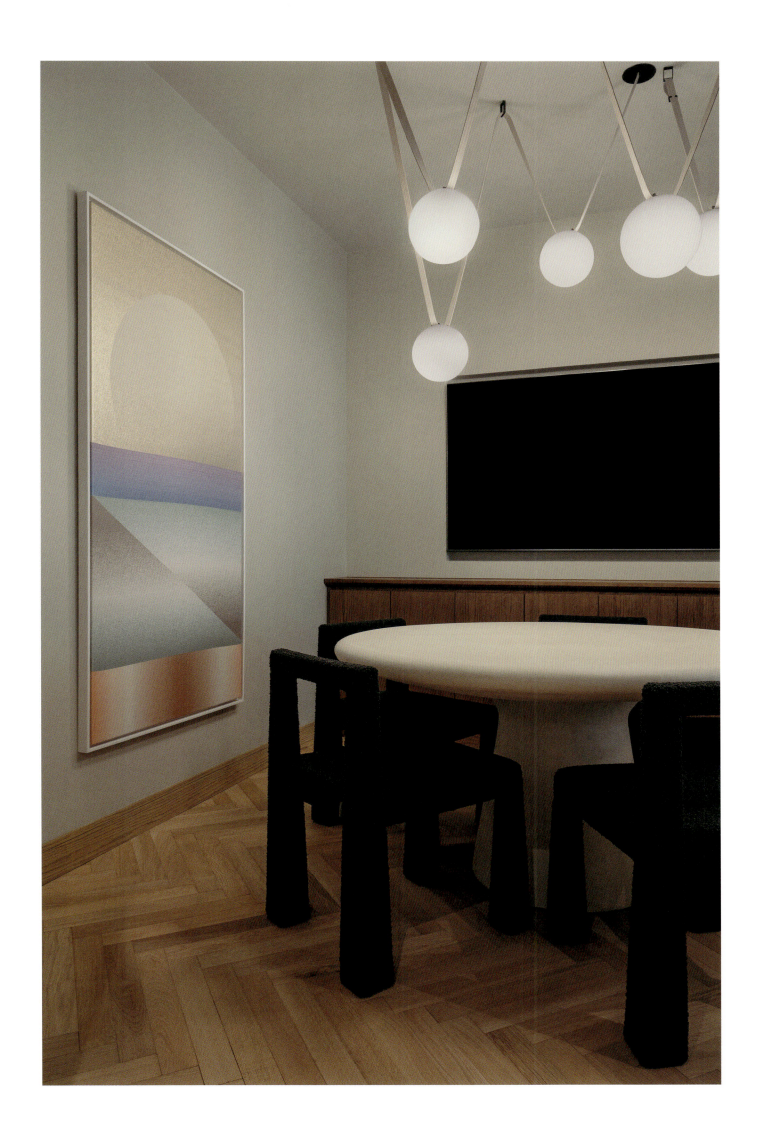

HI Projects Design Studio

Imagine a space as a haven of tranquility and functionality, tailored to the rhythm of your life. This is the essence of Hi Projects, a Dubai-based design studio specializing in creating timeless and livable interiors for residential and commercial projects across the GCC region.

The creative force behind Hi Projects Design Studio is Belgian Interior Designer Melissa Charlier, who has over 15 years of experience in crafting exceptional spaces. Melissa's signature style is a captivating blend of minimalist elegance, a soothing neutral color palette, and the artful integration of natural elements.

Hi Projects goes beyond aesthetics. Their approach emphasizes attention to detail and functionality. Every design decision, from the selection of materials to the placement of furniture and lighting design, is made with precision. This meticulousness ensures the creation of captivating interiors that stand the test of time.

The key to achieving timeless design lies in collaboration. Hi Projects fosters a strong partnership with each client. They work diligently to understand your story, lifestyle, and functional needs. Their philosophy revolves around transforming your vision into reality – a space that reflects the essence of who you are.

www.thehiprojects.com

Rixos Hotel Residence Apartment

Envision stepping into serene elegance, a world away from Dubai's vibrant energy. This recently renovated apartment within the Rixos Hotel Residence offers exactly that, boasting stunning panoramic views of the iconic Palm Jumeirah.

Originally a standard hotel apartment, the space has been transformed by the Hi Projects design team. They envisioned a haven for a young family, cleverly combining the kitchen and living area into a welcoming heart of the home. Warm wood tones create a sense of warmth and comfort, while subtle marble accents add a touch of sophistication. Picture cozy evenings spent together, laughter echoing in this inviting space.

The master bedroom is a private sanctuary, a place to unwind after a busy day. A cozy nook promises quiet moments with a good book, while the minimalist ensuite bathroom promotes a sense of tranquility and well-being.

This project is a testament to the design studio's philosophy. Here, practicality and aesthetics dance in perfect harmony. The seamlessly merged spaces ensure comfortable living for a young family, while the stylish touches elevate the everyday. This is not just an apartment; it's a serene oasis reflecting the vibrant spirit of Dubai, yet offering a refuge from its bustling pace.

Photography: Sergei Nekrasov

Abboud Malak

After an international upbringing and a successful career in Los Angeles, Abboud Malak established Studio M in 2007.

This award-winning, multidisciplinary interior design practice distinguishes itself with moody and immersive designs that Malak takes pleasure in creating. Each project is imbued with timeless mastery, forming unique relationships with clients to create spaces that go beyond aesthetics and fully engage people.

Studio M embodies a purist approach to design. Driven by human experience and enjoyable living, they recognize the pivotal role environment plays in daily lives.

They are passionate architects, interior designers, and furniture builders who believe in the power of space and its impact on human well-being.

Perpetually curious and forward-thinking, they approach each project without a formula, aiming to create spaces that elicit both visual novelty and authenticity.

While their philosophy remains consistent, every project inspires new ideas, investigations, and nuances.

Studio M is not a typical interior design consultancy. They believe in building close relationships with their clients, guiding them through the meticulous and ever-evolving design journey.

They are committed to the pragmatic and honest pursuit of inspiring and emotional spaces that resonate.

www.studiom.co

One Palm Residence 1403

Located on the trunk of Palm Jumeirah island, One Palm by Omniyat is an extraordinary project comprising 94 luxury apartments over 25 floors. Each apartment offers breathtaking views of the promenade, the iconic Burj Al Arab, and Dubai's magnificent skyline.

One Palm features various types of properties, including this Apartment 1403, designed by Studio M. With its modern and elegant design and neutral color décor, this residence boasts a spacious terrace with panoramic views of the Arabian Gulf. Featuring dramatic cantilevers with double and triple-height spaces, the interiors are designed to celebrate the effortless luxury of a beachside lifestyle. They come complete with ample natural light, outdoor spaces, and high-end materials and finishes.

Apartment 1403 by Studio M epitomizes these qualities. In response to the developer's brief to create a warm reinterpretation of modernism that resonates with a discerning and cosmopolitan clientele, Studio M envisioned a sanctuary that exudes effortless luxury living, relaxation, entertainment, and wellness. The floor-to-ceiling sliding glass windows retract to merge the interiors with the outdoor spaces, opening up to expansive terraces and entertainment areas. Maximizing views was a crucial consideration, and this is realized across all rooms of the residence, whether they overlook Dubai Marina, the Palm, or the open sea.

Elegant and comfortable, the residence is a model for living under the sun, fully embracing the richness of an indoor-outdoor lifestyle; Abboud Malak and his team collaborated closely with top industry professionals, including furniture and lighting designers. They are masters in their fields, and Abboud and Studio M gained valuable insights from working with them on this project.

All the various components, from the interiors to the landscaping, come together to celebrate and elevate the stunning surroundings of the property.

Photography: Oculis Project

Maryam Karji *Raha Milani*

archiSENSE

archiSENSE studio is an esteemed architecture and interior design practice located in Dubai.

Specializing in high-end residential projects, their boutique studio has earned a stellar reputation for delivering innovative and sustainable spaces that exceed their clients' expectations.

Established in 2018 by the dynamic duo of Maryam Karji, Founder and Managing Director of archiSENSE, and Raha Milani, co-Founder and Design Director, is a testament to the power of friendship and a shared vision.

Both graduated from the prestigious American University of Sharjah where Maryam studied Bachelor of Interior Architecture and Raha studied Bachelor of Architecture. They have seamlessly blended their expertise in architecture, interior architecture and landscape to create a studio that embodies a perfect harmony of contemporary design and cultural relevance.

As each project undertaken by archiSENSE unfolds, it becomes evident that their work is not merely about creating physical spaces, but about weaving a narrative that encapsulates the essence of their clients' stories. archiSENSE believes in the power of conversation between design, space and experience and how perceptibility of all these conversations is deeply dependent on the level of coherence and honesty of each.

The studio's unique approach ensures that every project resonates with a soul of its own, reflecting the individuality and aspirations of those it is designed for.

www.archisensestudio.com

House ar - Details Within Walls

House ar is a family private villa, located in Dubai.

The project is about materializing the experiences within the walls that completes the architecture and brings the spaces to life, connecting interior with exterior.

The scope of this project focuses on the interior architecture and design, within that, each zone and function of the house is analyzed with respect to the existing walls.

The interior design process was a treatment of unique elements that divide one space from another indirectly instead of using walls.

Hence, the spaces are designed cohesively in respect to the residents' needs, interaction, and experience.

Photography: Oculis Project

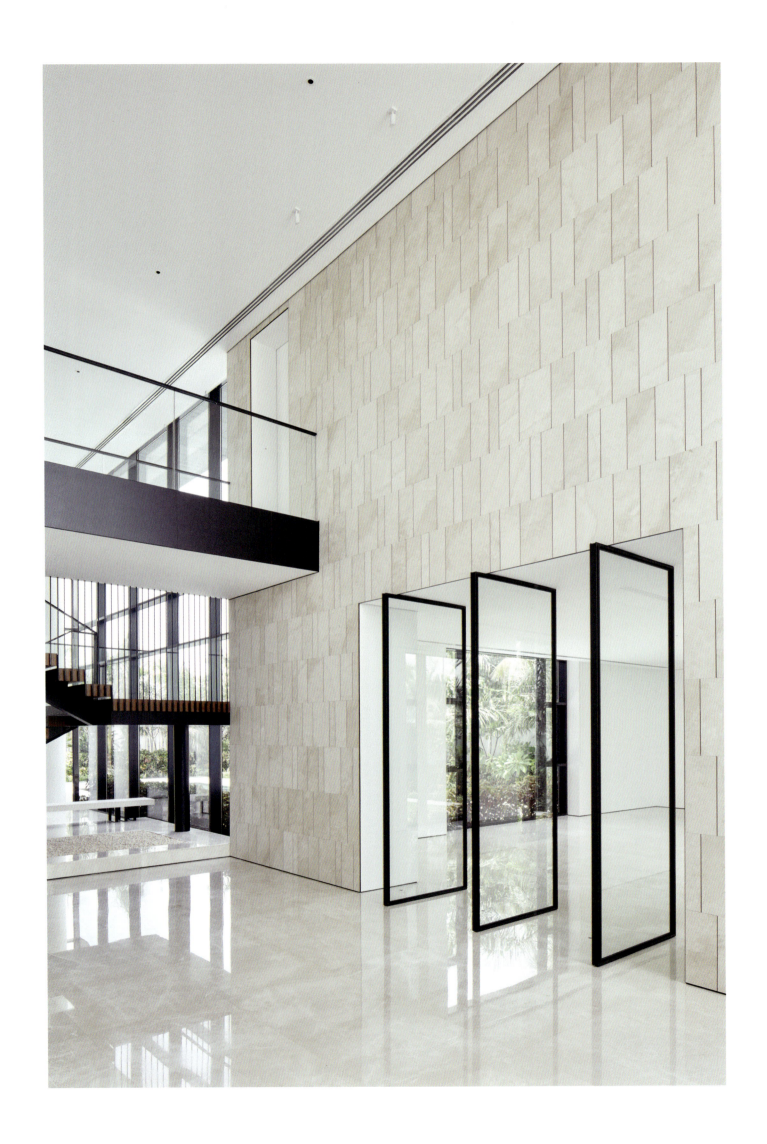

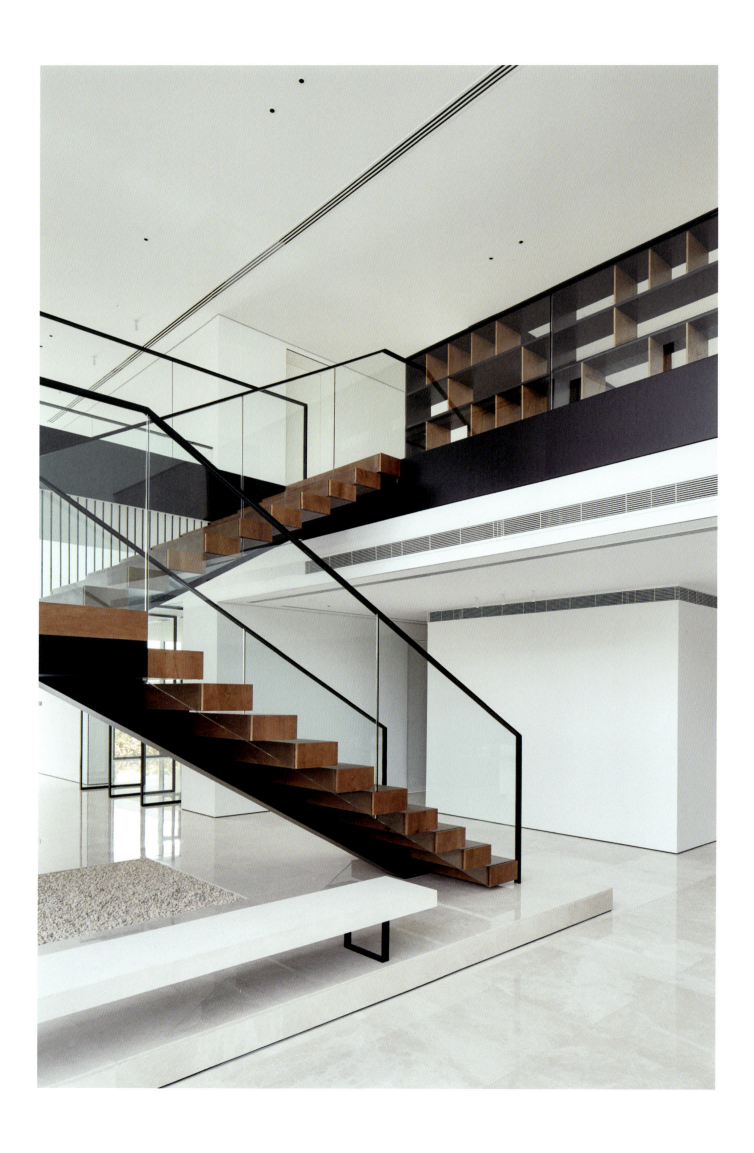

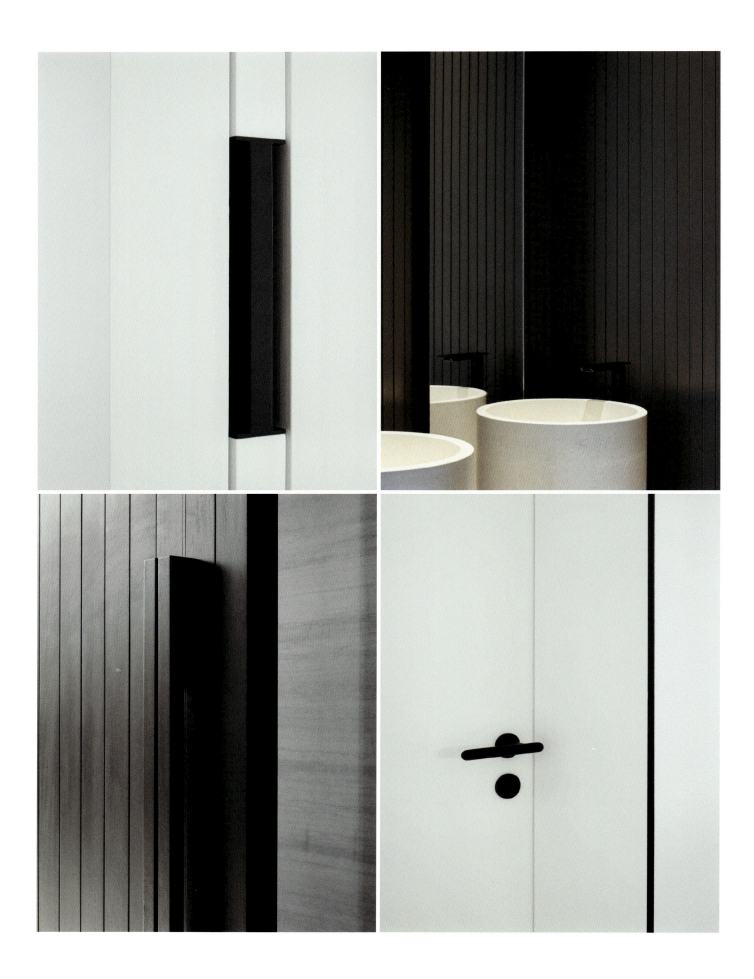

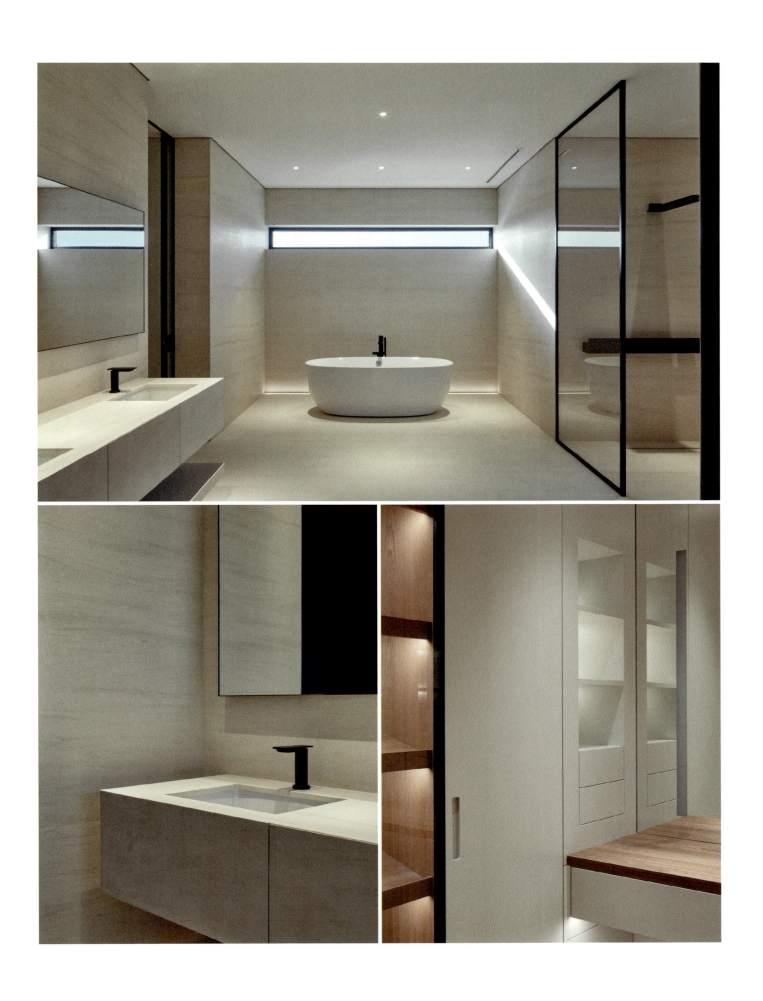

Rania M. Hamed
Principal Designer

VSHD Design

Interior Architect Rania M. Hamed, founder of the multiple award-winning boutique firm VSHD Design based in Dubai, is known for her innovative interiors and outstanding quality designs.

Hamed ensures her visualizations are not trend-led but synonymous with timelessness and longevity. Hamed's projects are based on strong design concepts and great attention to detail.

Transforming spaces through the creative use of light ensures both functional living and working environments throughout her designs.

Rania M. Hamed is fascinated by the challenge of integrating traditional culture and techniques into contemporary design and strives to introduce this dichotomy in her work.

VSHD Design believes that as both architects and interior design creatives, their role is to transform and repurpose spaces and breathe new life into them.

With each project, Rania and her team combine modesty with elegance to achieve elements of calm, beauty, and subtle luxury.

VSHD Design specializes in both residential and commercial spaces and has completed projects across the world, from Florida to London, Cairo, Amman, Dubai, and Abu Dhabi.

www.vshd.net

The Pool House

The Pool House by VSHD Design combines elegant, minimalist architecture with lush desert vegetation and the Arabian Sea's expansive views. Created to merge living and working spaces, it is especially relevant in the post-pandemic era, where home offices are in high demand.

The Pool House comprises three structures: two new edifices and one 15-year-old Mediterranean-style building. This juxtaposition adds vibrancy to the design. The one-level construction reflects the traditional homes of Emirati fishermen found along Jumeirah Beach, elevating them to a contemporary aesthetic. The main block includes a living and dining room, an outdoor kitchen, and a pool, while the secondary block houses a gym and a kids' majlis.

The client desired a modern living space for relaxation, work, and entertainment, separate from their main villa. The plot accommodates the two modern edifices surrounded by lush gardens, with a pool in between. The outdoor space, filled with greenery, links the blocks and is a defining trait of the structure. The design evokes a resort-like ambiance, emphasizing privacy and tranquility. VSHD Design aimed to create a resort-style abode, with direct street access and a walkway lined with greenery, enhancing the feeling of a secluded retreat. Each Alcove has its own entrance, adding to the sense of privacy and retreat.

Upon entering, visitors are greeted by lush greenery behind a glass wall, offering views of the second Alcove's patio with an olive tree. The first block features a living room, dining room, and open kitchen, connected by a corridor with a skylight and storage. This space is ideal for home life, entertaining, and work.

The second block resembles a health club, with a gym, multipurpose room, and spa. Large arched windows and earthy colors, with clay plaster walls and rough raw concrete floors, create a resilient indoor-outdoor space. Natural oak wood complements the resort vibe, with high-end, sophisticated furniture and accessories.

The design strives to evoke serenity through its architectural lines and interplay of light and shadow, creating a sense of calm and purity. The outdoor kitchen links the living and dining areas, offering an open space for intimate or large-scale entertaining. The Pool House provides a harmonious live/work environment amid calming natural surroundings.

Photography: Oculis Project

Vera Dieckmann
Creative Director XO Atelier

Augustine Wong

XO Atelier
Augustine Wong

XO Atelier is an avant-garde interior design studio with a profound commitment to redefining hospitality spaces. Through a unique blend of contemporary aesthetics and timeless sensibilities, XO Atelier creates environments that engage, inspire, and transport patrons to new realms of luxury and sophistication.

With a portfolio spanning international collaborations and groundbreaking designs, XO Atelier continues to reshape the boundaries of interior design within the hospitality industry.

Creative Director & Founder Vera Edith Dieckmann established XO Atelier in December 2020 in Dubai to fulfill the breadth of her creative potential in the field of design. She is a graduate engineer in architecture with over 26 years of experience across all areas of interior design and architecture.

Working for renowned practices including David Ling in New York, Gunther Spitzley in Zurich, Matteo Thun Studio in Milan, and DWP Malaysia, Vera also honed her skills at global hospitality chains Marriott Holdings and FRHI (now ACCOR) as Director of Design. Driven by her desire to discover a unique path, Vera launched her studio to offer clients the support and dedicated services they need.

XO Atelier has unleashed an extraordinary marvel in the heart of Dubai—a sanctuary that fuses the vibrant pulse of the city with an Asian-inspired narrative, all meticulously curated to epitomize the essence of contemporary elegance.

In a captivating synthesis of design and cultural heritage, XO Atelier has conjured an interior for Augustine Wong, a client whose Asian roots demanded a fresh perspective on modern minimalism. The result? An environment that marries understated sophistication with function, crafting an experience that's both aesthetic and pragmatic.

www.xo-atelier.net

A Minimalist Sanctuary in Dubai

Bridging tradition and innovation, Vera Dieckmann embarked on a journey with Augustine Wong to manifest his aspirations. The outcome is a symphony of modernism, elegance, and Wong's distinctive flair. Dieckmann's impeccable precision with geometric elements and clean lines creates a canvas of tranquility that echoes Wong's personal narrative.

At the heart of this masterpiece is a contemporary story, illuminated by a gentle spectrum of creams and off-whites. This understated palette forms the foundation upon which the sanctuary's identity is built, providing respite from the frenzy of Wong's dynamic schedule.

As the sun orchestrates its daily performance, the scene transforms. Architectural lighting, meticulously curated by Nemo Lighting, engages in a dance of light and shadow, breathing life into Latifa Saeed's integrated artworks. This symphony of luminescence interacts with the linear cove lights and concealed fixtures, choreographing an ever-evolving visual spectacle within the space.

One of the sanctuary's remarkable features is the water-rippled, high-polished steel surface gracing the living room's window-framed bench seating. This design marvel, akin to nature's aqueous poetry, mirrors dancing reflections and shadows, evoking a metamorphic atmosphere that mirrors the sun's passage.

The XO Atelier team's ingenuity shines in the ensuite master bathroom, where a rippled glass wall - reminiscent of Asian paravent screens - merges the space with the bedroom, gifting the former with newfound dimensions and the latter with an elaborate infusion of natural light.

Draped in luxurious engineered travertine tiles from the esteemed Spanish brand Inalco, the bathroom becomes an oasis adorned with matte black faucets. A wooden paravent veils the neighboring urban tapestry, encapsulating an air of Asian mystique. Each element was handpicked to harmonize with the design, including built-in furniture meticulously aligned with Wong's vision and the overarching minimalist aesthetic.

Reflecting Wong's fervor for design and literary marvels, hand-selected loose furniture punctuates the space, subtly adding his signature touch. Through an ensemble of literature and design artifacts, Wong's distinctive essence is woven seamlessly into the sanctuary's fabric.

Vera Dieckmann encapsulates XO Atelier's ethos with precision, stating that she likes places to be functional, uncluttered, and sleek. This philosophy stands as a testament to the firm's commitment to modern design and the art of seamlessly integrating opulence without ostentation.

Beyond the artistry and precision, the sanctuary offers respite within Dubai's ceaseless rhythm. It beckons as an oasis of elegance and character, where urbane allure coalesces with serenity—an embodiment of refined living in the modern age.

XO Atelier's architectural masterpiece embodies their signature: a fusion of modernism and sleek lines, enlivening simplicity with elegance and warmth. This transcendent sanctuary speaks of XO Atelier's vision - a realm where form dances effortlessly with function, inviting Augustine Wong to his urban haven, seamlessly woven within Dubai's dynamic tapestry.

Photography: Natelee Cocks

Eyad Zarafeh
Co-Founder / Project Director

Pariya Manafi
Co-Founder / Creative Director

NAQSH Architecture

NAQSH Architecture is a comprehensive design and architecture studio dedicated to creating remarkable experiences - one unique space at a time, with impeccable attention to detail in Dubai, the UAE, and beyond.

Whether clients are looking to transform their dream home or open a new fusion cafe, they can rely on NAQSH Architecture's 25+ years of expertise, signature process, and G+4 license to bring their vision to life.

From bespoke homes to upscale hotels, charming cafes, and distinct commercial spaces, NAQSH Architecture provides comprehensive architectural, interior design, and engineering solutions, supporting clients through every phase of their project.

They aim to blend form and function in every design without compromising individual lifestyle, values, and style preferences. Whether it's a moment of calm over a cup of coffee or dinner with a growing family, their team will design a concept that combines the elegance of the client's chosen aesthetic with thoughtful solutions for a safe and enjoyable environment for the whole family.

They understand the importance of first impressions in commercial spaces. That's why they work closely with clients to determine how they want a space to look, feel, and function from the moment customers or clients step inside. Whether it's the allure of an exquisite resort or the distinctive character of a new restaurant in the heart of the city, they ensure every detail is considered to make each space even better than envisioned.

With over 50 projects successfully completed, NAQSH Architecture has transformed unique spaces ranging from modern villas and luxury apartments to boutique resorts, restaurants, performance halls, and more.

www.naqsharchitecture.com

Break Al Qana

Break Al Qana, completed by NAQSH in December 2023, is situated in Al Qana, Abu Dhabi. NAQSH Architecture handled the interior design and construction supervision for this signature project.

Nestled in Abu Dhabi's vibrant waterfront district, Break offers a unique twist on all-day dining, transforming its culinary creations into captivating art pieces.

To set itself apart from its sister company, Mara, Break blends contemporary elegance with whimsical charm - featuring custom statement chandeliers, intricately patterned floors, and live pastry and pizza-making displays.

Large windows seamlessly connect the indoor and outdoor spaces, enhancing the culinary experience. Guests can enjoy a variety of seating options surrounded by lush greenery, with strategically placed logos guiding their attention to the main entrance and pizza counter.

Photography: Natelee Cocks

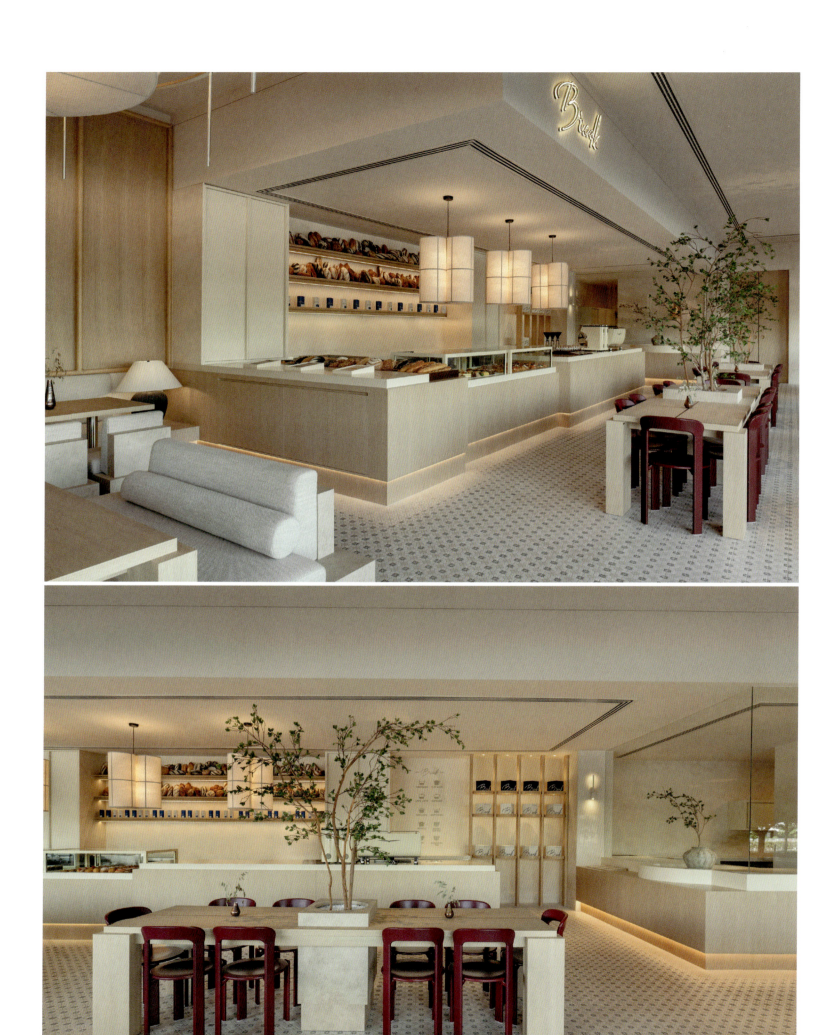

Hana Hakim

British-born Syrian Hana Hakim is a multi-award-winning interior designer and the founder of The Stella Collective.

Her ability to infuse light and space into her work has led to commissions both locally and internationally, ranging from elegant workspaces that embody well-being to some of Australia's most prolific and iconic restaurants. Framing these spaces and volumes with extreme precision, her design is known for having a timeless quality that touches the human core.

Hana Hakim's philosophy is to create goodness in this world, in our environment, whether it be a vibrant hotel, a hospitality venue, a workplace that embodies well-being, or even a small village in Palestine.

Hana and her team create spaces that make people feel good. They design with love, truth, and fearlessness.

A number of brands, restaurants, luxury retail houses, workspaces, and private residences have been marked with the "Stella Seal of Loose Luxury," embodying Hana's signature of elegant clean lines, light-filled tranquility, and voluminous splendor.

The Stella Collective (est. 2015) is Hana's pride, joy, and life's work. Her passion for breathing life into businesses, buildings, and a feel-good culture through design with her team is unrivaled. Each job, regardless of size, takes shape after a deep research period, delving into space, ambiance, context, and history... and most importantly, the clients' narrative.

A unique mantra exists within the culture and company she has built at Stella. Each project is a tribute to travel, opening one's heart to adventure, memories, and powerful storytelling.

Hana is internationally recognized with distinctive design awards and numerous publications and design accolades over almost twenty years of experience, including Phaidon's book "The World's Best Contemporary Interior Designers," making exceptional, innovative, and groundbreaking contributions to design.

www.thestellacollective.co

Casa Amal, Dubai

Situated in Dubai's Al Wasl neighborhood, Casa Amal is an architectural masterpiece that intersects traditional orientalism, Arabian modernism, and slow luxury.

Casa Amal is steeped in rich cultural heritage and modernity, drawing inspiration from the 1970s Arabian modernist era in Dubai and the Emirates region—a period that marked the beginning of a modern renaissance in architecture and thought. Beyond its architecture, Casa Amal is a sacred space exuding an aura of love, purity, and light.

Characterized by sandy hues, delicate perforations, and light-filled spaces, this contemporary dwelling reflects the historic land it inhabits. Designed by the Australian-based practice The Stella Collective, Casa Amal upholds the studio's ethos that design should be local to its surroundings. As a calming sanctuary, it is an elegant tapestry of interior and exterior spaces that coalesce at premeditated intervals.

The custom clay arched breeze blocks on the facade are a modernist reimagining of traditional mashrabiya - wooden lattice screens found in traditional Arabic architecture. These elements provide ventilation and views while projecting an ever-changing mosaic of sunlight and shadows throughout the day. Other nods to mashrabiya include the perforated travertine wall behind the staircase and the honeycomb doors leading to the gardens, which together allow nature to be an active participant in the design.

The linear nature of the architecture is counterbalanced by curving walls and five-meter-high arches that pay homage to Moorish architecture. The Stella Collective combined traditional render with Italian travertine for the facade, creating a monolithic appearance that changes color as the day progresses. Strategic use of greenery enhances the overall lush, escapist experience, with a similar approach applied to the bathrooms, featuring tiled mosaic vanities.

When it came to the palette, The Stella Collective exercised tactful restraint. Hakim and her team chose soulful light play, comfortable clean lines, monumental proportions, and textured, soothing finishes. The palette borrows from nature, channeling a golden glow that complements the natural light. Sand-toned travertine warms the floor, while olive green mosaic tiles adorn an array of bathroom fixtures. The mood is of effortless luxury. It's deeply rooted in orientalism but without being overly themed. It breaks free from tradition while still echoing a sense of modern, oriental-chic elegance.

The home's centerpiece is a summer courtyard with a swimming pool. No room is secluded; all rooms have a visual connection to the garden oasis surrounding the property through perforated screens or steel-framed glass doors.

Architecture and Interior Design: The Stella Collective. Build: Emirates Sands Contracting and Al Araya Engineering Consultants. Landscape design: Kamelia Landscape Design.

Photography: Lillie Thompson

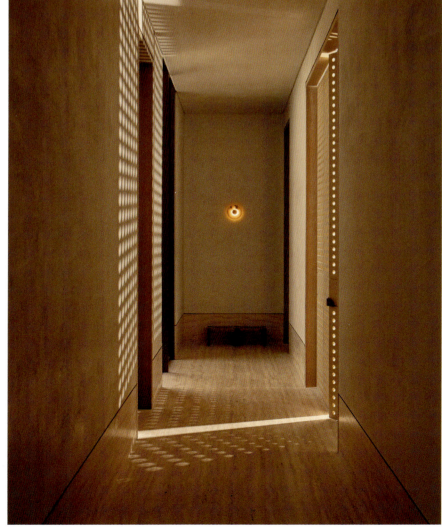

Portrait by J.C. Carbonne

Kengo Kuma

Kengo Kuma was born in 1954. He established Kengo Kuma & Associates (KKAA) in 1990.

He is currently a University Professor and Professor Emeritus at the University of Tokyo after teaching at Keio University and the University of Tokyo. KKAA projects are currently underway in more than 50 countries.

Kengo Kuma proposes architecture that opens up new relationships between nature, technology, and human beings.

His major publications include Zen Shigoto (Kengo Kuma – the complete works, Daiwa Shobo), Ten Sen Men ("point, line, plane", Iwanami Shoten), Makeru Kenchiku (Architecture of Defeat, Iwanami Shoten), Shizen na Kenchiku (Natural Architecture, Iwanami Shinsho), Chii-sana Kenchiku (Small Architecture, Iwanami Shinsho) and many others.

Kengo Kuma & Associates have offices in Tokyo, Paris, Beijing, Shanghai and Seoul.

www.kkaa.co.jp

St Regis Red Sea Resort, Saudi Arabia

Kengo Kuma's design approach for the Ummahat AlShaykh island project, situated in the Red Sea, is deeply rooted in the site's unique characteristics, fostering a philosophy of seamless integration with the surrounding landscape.

Despite the challenges presented by the delicate environment, their site-specific approach guided them in crafting low, horizontally oriented Land Villas with gently curved roofs, mirroring the natural sand dunes. This design not only ensures guest privacy but also harmonizes with the island's topography, minimizing sand infill and preserving its natural shape.

The arrangement of buildings on the land follows the natural profile and geometry of the shoreline, incorporating curved organic shapes to blend harmoniously with the desert landscape. Inspired by the rich coral life within the island's oceans, their design for the offshore sea villas features a spiral volume emerging gracefully from the sea, offering unobstructed views of the ocean landscape. All structures, including hotel facilities, embrace a coral and dune-shaped plan, reflecting their commitment to integrating architecture with its environment.

In terms of material selection, they aimed to minimize the use of concrete and instead employed prefabrication systems, primarily incorporating wood and clay plaster to infuse warmth and tenderness into the architecture. Spruce wood, selected for its durability in the highly saline environment, complements clay plaster, which reflects the patterns of sand dunes and natural weathering processes, thereby emphasizing the buildings' connection to nature.

The roofs are clad with natural cedar wood shingles, renowned for their natural beauty and resilience against harsh weather conditions. Their design ethos embodies a holistic approach to architecture, seamlessly merging with the environment while prioritizing sustainability and durability.

Architecture: Kengo Kuma & Associates. Construction: Blumer-Lehmann AG.

Photography: Nicola Maniero

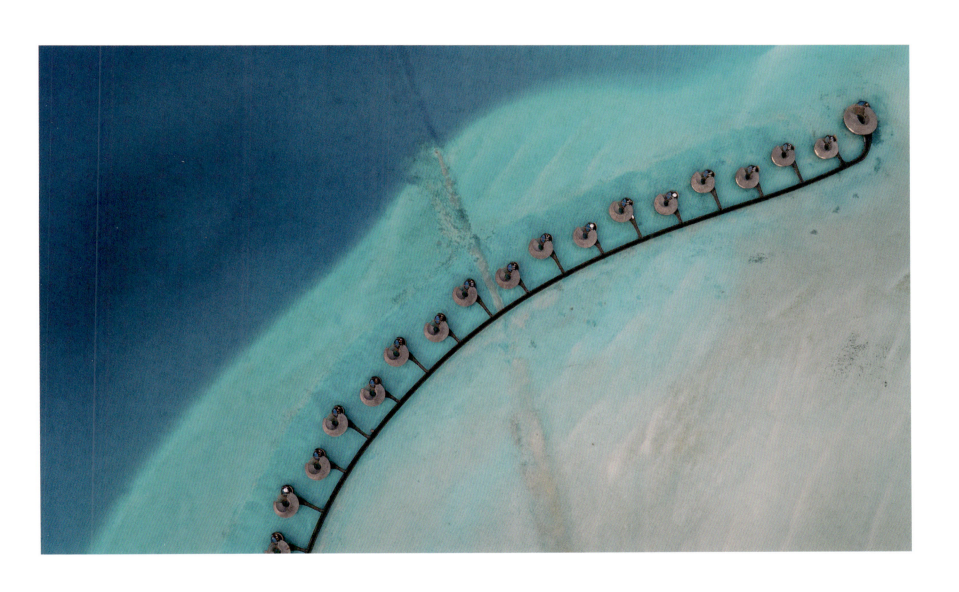

Custom No.9

Founded by Amy Durnford, Custom No.9 is a retail and contract furniture brand, with an in-house design studio and a curated collection of customizable designs.

They offer furniture for Hospitality, F&B, Leisure, Retail, and direct-to-consumer markets.

Established in 2019, they were born with a vision to introduce a new realm of customized furniture to the Middle East market by offering a truly design-led approach.

They produce original designs with an edge that celebrate expression, individuality, and an unwavering commitment to quality and craftsmanship.

A mix of angular, rounded, and geometric shapes combined with nostalgic materials make up their collections.

While bold in their own way, they are all rooted in a simplistic ethos.

www.customno9.com

Casa Maya

Custom No.9 designer Amy Durnford has envisioned an ethereal haven with the help of the UAE's finest artisans. Her favorite space, the sunken conversation pit, is bathed in natural light from the large windows and bespoke bi-folding doors she installed on the right. Despite the tricky layout and other technical challenges common with old villas in Dubai, the couple fell in love with the 20-meter-tall trees embracing the site. Earthy textures like linen, jute, and ceramics enhance the home's natural vibe.

Over eight months, they demolished almost all non-structural internal walls and replaced the original 2007 bathrooms and kitchen. The existing kitchen was gutted to create a seamless social space for cooking, hosting, and everyday living.

This vision required significant modifications, including enclosing the first-floor balcony to expand the principal bedroom, adding split levels, and adapting the porch to create a home office. Inspired by their time in Mexico, they created an ambiance by rendering all surfaces in the same finish and installing geometric flooring to disguise the modest proportions of the guest ensuite.

Amy developed every design element that gives the house its distinct character, collaborating with fellow UAE businesses. From the T-bar door handles and pivoting bifold panels that open the living space to the outdoors, to the micro-cement finish that flows from the walls and floors onto the curved kitchen island, these elements give the home its earthy look. She often pushed suppliers to try new techniques, resulting in high-quality workmanship such as the hand-bent metal rail of the jute-floored stairwell and rounded edges that lend softness to the interior architecture.

Photography: Natelee Cocks

The Etereo team

Stefania Digregorio and Mirko Sala Tenna, founders of Etereo

Etereo

Etereo is the story of an Italian studio with Middle Eastern charm, narrated by two designers and artists united by a single vision. Stefania Digregorio and Mirko Sala Tenna founded their Architectural and Interior Design Studio in 2017, with headquarters in the United Arab Emirates and a second business division in Milan.

Etereo, true to the meaning of its name, evokes a concept of spiritual nature. Their focus on the human scale, in harmony with aesthetic beauty, is at the core of every project they undertake.

The pursuit of inner well-being drives them to transcend the tangible boundaries of matter and space, which become tools for Etereo to achieve a sublime, immersive experience. It's a sensory journey, harmonized with nature and the slow passage of time - that is Etereo.

The atelier offers consultancy for architectural projects, interior design, and product development, drawing on influences from the Italian artistic heritage and the richness of the Middle East, all united with passion. Their meticulous approach encompasses art direction, material and finish selection, sourcing from top suppliers, and the execution of every detail, exemplifying virtuosity. Etereo specializes in luxury projects, including residential properties, exclusive hospitality, yachting, and refined commercial spaces, catering to a global market with a focus on Europe, the Middle East, and Asia.

Etereo was born from the founders' desire to blend the sophistication of Italian architecture and design with the influences of Dubai's lunar landscape, creating a unique material fusion. Mirko Sala Tenna's innovative perspective, shaped by his Alpine heritage and futuristic outlook, along with Stefania Digregorio's talent for infusing contemporary flair while honoring past artistic traditions, have established the Made in Italy atelier as a symbol of excellence in Dubai.

www.etereodesign.it

Burj Khalifa Rubino Penthouse

Etereo is renowned for seamlessly blending luxury with meticulous craftsmanship, creating spaces that are both sophisticated and functional. Their recent projects, such as the Burj Khalifa Rubino Penthouse in Dubai, embody this vision, showcasing the pinnacle of refined living through the use of high-quality materials and innovative design.

The Burj Khalifa Rubino Penthouse, situated on the 103rd floor of Dubai's iconic Burj Khalifa, stands as a testament to luxury and meticulous design. This 4,494-square-foot penthouse exemplifies sophistication, characterized by carefully selected materials, mostly sourced from Italian partners, and a keen attention to detail. Upon entry, visitors are greeted by fabric wallpaper with sinuous forms running along almost the entire perimeter. The floor and surrounding walls feature full-height camouflage marble, creating a seamless connection with Dubai's external beauty.

The corridors, adorned with large pivot doors clad in marble, lead to various spaces, imparting a sense of grandeur and privacy. The spacious living area is a harmonious blend of elegance and dynamism, with large structural columns hidden by red-orange leather that define the space. The circular living area, with dark parquet flooring, encircles a cozy dining area featuring soft lines, a marble dining table, and glass chandeliers. Adjacent is a relaxation area designed with a magnificent white grand piano.

The custom-made, freestanding bar counter is adorned with bronze metal and a Calacatta violet marble top, complemented by a temperature-controlled cellar behind large glass doors. Curved sliding doors with fabric wallpaper reveal well-hidden functional spaces, maintaining design continuity and offering a panoramic view of the Dubai skyline, framed by motorized curtains that elegantly cover the entire window span. The kitchen, a masterpiece almost entirely made of black marble, features countertops, backsplashes, and cabinets, with blue-green metal and bronze retractable doors revealing hidden amenities.

The master bedroom and bathroom redefine luxury with a curved grey oak vanity table, greige Travertine marble, and Forest brown marble details, an open wardrobe with dark parquet flooring, and fabric wallpaper. Each bedroom is a sanctuary with leather-clad walls, each featuring different themes to create a unique and personalized atmosphere. In the Burj Khalifa Rubino project, luxury is not just a visual spectacle but an immersive experience, where every detail contributes to the narrative of one of Dubai's most prestigious addresses.

Photography: Oculis Project

The three partners of MMA Projects (from left to right): Alessandro Vaghi, Dorotea De Simone and the founder of the studio, Marco Mangili

MMA Projects

MMA Projects is a multidisciplinary and multicultural architecture and design studio based in Milan.

MMA Projects works internationally in multiple sectors, from residential to commercial, and from retail to hospitality.

The team is driven by passion and united in the pursuit of beauty and excellence. Rooted in the finest traditions of Italian design, MMA Projects declares its love for craftsmanship and customization.

Special emphasis is placed on the use of natural materials for their tactile qualities and their ability to give a building a sense of soul.

The result is the development of projects blending functionality and poetry, technical skills, and aesthetic sophistication.

A unique vision where forms are reduced to their essence, color palettes are soft, and harmony and balance are the ultimate goals.

www.mmaprojects.com

Villa ABK

In MMA Project's impressive portfolio, Villa ABK stands out: an enchanting private residence, a sculptural villa where the interplay of double-height volumes and skylight reflections define the internal architectural spaces in a dance of light and shadow, solid and void. This 4,000-square-meter villa is located on the prestigious Pearl Jumeirah Island, near one of Dubai's trendiest locations, the Nikki Beach Hotel & Resort, offering unparalleled sea views.

The concept aims to maximize the openness of internal spaces, creating a horizontal and vertical continuum emphasized by the main partitions. These internal divisions not only define the floor plan but also accentuate the residential volume's strong verticality. This results in open living spaces where functions flow seamlessly, allowing light and nature to become integral parts. Villa ABK is a tailor-made residence, like a bespoke suit tailored to the client's needs. The project imparts uniqueness and identity to the environment, with volumes and chiaroscuro themes blending seamlessly.

The ground floor houses the heart of the home, a vast open space overlooking the sea where all representative activities take place. This formal area includes a majlis, a place of hospitality and Arab conviviality. The ground floor also features a second living area, a dining area, and a dramatic double-height kitchen. The choice of material shades, including marble, wood, and brushed brass, creates an enveloping chromatic harmony. There's also a dedicated formal workspace for the family, providing a tranquil corner for concentration.

Externally, the villa is clad in white Turkish stone called Limra, treated with various finishes, creating surface contrast between the lower and upper parts of the building. The lower section features geometric bas-relief motifs, while the upper surface has a more delicate finish, resembling a woven pattern.

Inside, the residence deliberately showcases various stone texture treatments. This material versatility allows the same stone to display different color shades and reflections, a skillful play of light and shadow. The luxurious residence greets its guests with an elegant and voluminous Arabescato Orobico wall. The 9-meter-high entrance Synua door by OIKOS is made with bronze finishes and an external engineered wood covering.

For the interior cladding, three predominant materials are used: grey Fior di Bosco marble and Verde Antigua marble, chosen for their unique colors and veining, contrasted with Canaletto Walnut wood for the wainscoting. The outdoor area of the residence is characterized by Basalto Grigio stone, combined with large matte white ceramic slabs. White dominates the external architecture, while the interior blends subtle and light shades of grey and green, contrasted with warm wood tones.

Double-height spaces and large windows ensure natural brightness throughout the environment, complemented by the presence of dramatic chandeliers. The natural light entering through the windows guarantees captivating plays of light and shadow in the main hall, with luminous effects reflecting on the staircase wall, emphasizing the stone «blade» motif found throughout the home. The villa also features a comprehensive home automation system.

The rational interplay of volumes and textures becomes the source of inspiration for the external facades, defining their forms and structure. The thin, lightweight slabs that compose them incorporate decorative bas-reliefs that, when exposed to sunlight, create unique and evocative light effects.

Photography: Natelee Cocks

A Tribute
to the Best
Architecture & Interior Photographers
in the Middle East

تكريم لأفضل مصوري العمارة والتصميم الداخلي في الشرق الأوسط

"Space and light and order. These are considered by designers when creating an interior space. I embrace each space in its intended light and aim to convey a feeling of order in my images."

Natelee Cocks, **Photographer**

Natelee Cocks

Natelee Cocks is an accomplished Dubai-based, interior, design and architecture photographer, with over 10 years of experience.

She started her photography journey in South Africa when she won an internship at a well respected wedding photography company. Her talent was soon noticed and only after a few months became one of their lead photographers. After moving to Dubai her horizons were broadened by the incredible design and architecture that UAE has to offer. Natelee Cocks Photography was born, and she quickly earned the reputation as one of the most sought-after photographers in the region.

She has a clean, minimalistic style and attention to intimate details. Her love and focus is incorporating natural light, interesting lines and textures. Natelee has been commissioned by some of the biggest names in the architecture and design industry and her award winning images have been featured in numerous international publications. Her talent has seen her work in some exotic locations, which is a perfect marriage for her love of traveling and exploring.

Quietly yet deeply expressive, her photography captures the essence of spaces, places, objects and moods.

Featured in this book on pages 42-55, 56-69, 140-153, 154-161, 192-205, 222-247, and 245.

www.nateleecocks.com

"Class and Good Taste are always in Style."

Oculis Project, Photographers

Oculis Project

Oculis Project: Nikola and Tamara, traditionally trained architects, are a husband-and-wife photography duo based in Dubai, UAE.

Through their lenses, they capture the objects, architecture, and people around them. Their photography is enhanced by their deep understanding of architecture, design, and culture. What started as a mutual hobby has grown into a professional collaboration over the years.

When you meet the couple behind the lens, you are greeted by two hardworking, good-natured, and detail-oriented individuals.

They combine their exceptional photography skills with a desire to understand the products, people, and spaces they capture, ensuring that their work reflects not only their vision but also that of their clients.

When not working, Nikola and Tamara enjoy sipping coffee or tasting wine, with their cameras always close by to document their experiences and share them with the rest of us.

Featured in this book on pages 2, 6-21, 22-41, 96-109, 110-123, 124-139, 206-221, front and back cover.

www.oculisproject.com

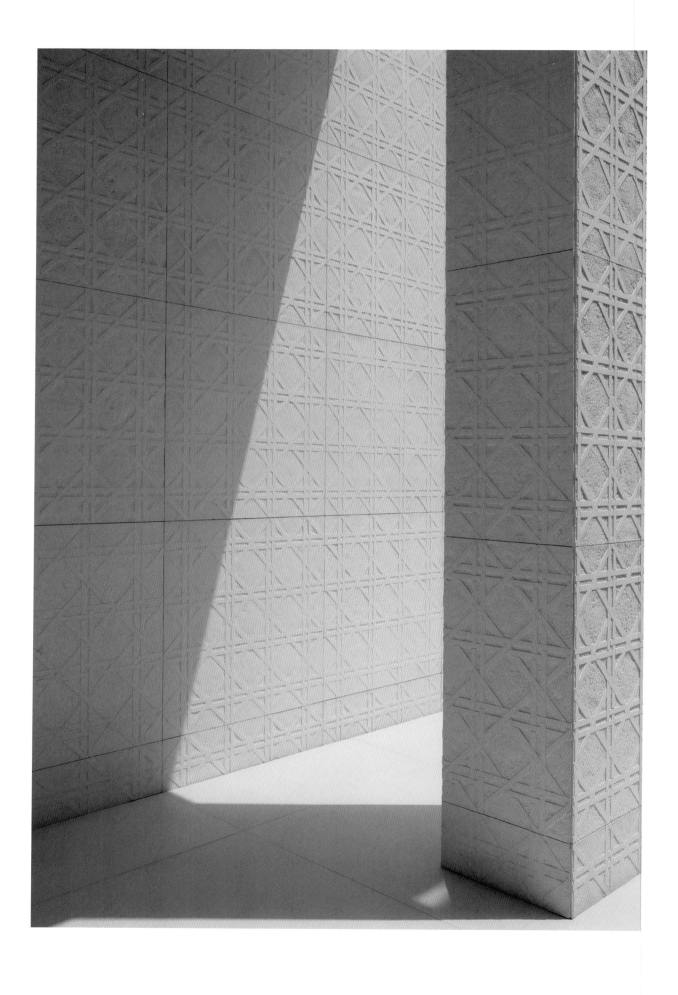

Acknowledgments
الشكر والتقدير

The Publisher wishes to thank:

• All owners of the wonderful private residences, resorts, and restaurants for their hospitality;

• All photographers for their excellent work (in order of appearance): Oculis Project, Natelee Cocks, Sergei Nekrasov, Lillie Thompson, Nicola Maniero;

• All portrait photographers (in order of appearance): Oscar Munart, Anna Maria Nielsen, J.C. Carbonne;

• Miriam Llano (Amphora) for her Foreword;

• All designers and architects who have participated in this book (in order of appearance): Erika & Giorgia Giacuzzo (Giacuzzo Design Studio), David Lessard & Stas Louca (H+A), Neeshay Nouman (The Niche Corner), Tristan Du Plessis, Melissa Charlier (HI Projects Design Studio), Frederico Cruz, Abboud Malak (Studio M), Maryam Karji & Raha Milani (archiSENSE), Rania M. Hamed (VSHD Design), Vera Dieckmann (XO Atelier) & Augustine Wong, Eyad Zarafeh & Pariya Manafi (NAQSH Architecture), Hana Hakim, Kengo Kuma, Amy Durnford (Custom No.9), Stefania Digregorio & Mirko Sala Tenna (Etereo), Alessandro Vaghi, and Dorotea De Simone & Marco Mangili (MMA Projects).

PUBLISHER
BETA-PLUS nv/sa
Avenue Louise 367
B-1050 Brussels
www.betaplus.com

DESIGN
Patrick Pierre

© 2024, BETA-PLUS

All rights reserved.

No parts of this publication may be reproduced,
stored in a retrieval system, or transmitted
in any form or by any means.

Printed in Belgium.